NAKED WITH SUMMER IN YOUR MOUTH

Naked With Summer in Your Mouth

poems by

Al Purdy

M&S

Canadian Cataloguing in Publication Data

Purdy, Al, 1918-
Naked with summer in your mouth

ISBN 0-7710-7221-X

I. Title.

PS8531.U74N3 1994   c811'.54   C94-931551-6
PR9199.3.P87N3 1994

The publishers acknowledge the support of the Canada
Council and the Ontario Arts Council for their publishing
program.

Typesetting by M&S, Toronto.
The support of the Government of Ontario through the
Ministry of Culture, Tourism and Recreation is acknowledged.

Printed and bound in Canada on acid-free paper.

McClelland & Stewart Inc.
The Canadian Publishers
481 University Avenue
Toronto, Ontario
M5G 2E9

1 2 3 4 5   98 97 96 95 94

For Eurithe

CONTENTS

GROSSE ISLE

Look, stranger, at this island now
The leaping light for your delight discovers –

– W.H. Auden

Look stranger
a diseased whale in the St. Lawrence
this other island than Auden's
dull grey when the weather is dull grey
and an east wind brings rain
this Appalachian outcrop
a stone ship foundered in the river estuary
now in the care and keeping of Parks Canada
– a silence here like no mainland silence
at Cholera Bay where the dead bodies
awaited high tide and the rough kindness
of waves sweeping them into the dark –

Look stranger
at this other island
weedgrown graves in the three cemeteries
be careful your clothes don't get hooked
by wild raspberry canes and avoid the poison ivy
– here children went mad with cholera fever
and raging with thirst they ran into the river
their parents following a little way
before they died themselves
– and don't stumble over the rusted tricycle
somehow overlooked at the last big cleanup
or perhaps left where it is for the tourists?

Look stranger
where the sea wind sweeps westward

down the estuary
this way the other strangers came
potato-famine Irish and Scotch crofters
refugees from the Highland clearances
and sailing ships waited here
to remove their corpses
and four million immigrants passed through
– now there's talk of a Health Spa and Casino
we could situate our billboard
right under the granite cross by the river:
        UNLIMITED INVESTMENT OPPORTUNITIES

Look stranger
see your own face reflected in the river
stumble up from the stinking hold
blinded by sunlight and into the leaky dinghy
only half-hearing the sailors taunting you
        "Shanty Irish! Shanty Irish!"
gulp the freshening wind and pinch yourself
trying to understand if the world is a real place
stumble again and fall when you reach the shore
and bless this poisoned earth
but stranger no longer
for this is home

"Gus" I said to Ralph Gustafson
– "here in Russki-land you indited
nineteen pomes I writ only eleven
so let us be true prosodic comrades
let us balance this disproportion
I'll trade you one of mine
for five of yours
that oughta be a fair trade besides
I am well-known for my generosity"
Gus looks a mite peculiar
then turns me down flat
I can't understand it
I mean his selfish attitude

"Gus" I said as we stood
in Red Square on sore feet waiting
weeks to get inside Lenin's tomb
and St. Basil's candy-coloured spires
dreaming among the nightmare guns
"Gus" I said "– if I trade you eleven
pomes for three by Pasternak
a sprig of orange mountain ash
from his house at Peredelkino
and the Boris troika for one by
Mayakovsky or two by Pushkin
and exchange those to Voznesensky
along with Tretiak's good goal stick
and a puck to Voz for his pomes
on Oza and Mayakovsky's Typist
and I give you these in exchange

plus a quarter-full litre of vodka
do I get the okay for your nineteen?"

("Take your hands outa your pockets
capitalistic swine" the Russki guard ordered
near Lenin's tomb and I did so)

Well it was a good try anyhow
the barter system does work sometimes
I figure even here in Russki-land
it's share and share alike besides
approaching Pasternak Pushkin Mayakovsky
and Voznesensky's Oza with a proposition
like this for my mutual betterment
is as close to greatness as I'm likely
to get given my modest abilities
And when we shuffled past his tomb
as if all us serfs were wearing leg irons
pale Vladimir Ilych had nothing to say
which I took to be silent agreement
but now considering my increased total
of pomes I should approach Blok's "The Twelve"
"How about it Gus?"

Moscow

PARTINGS

Nelson to Lady Hamilton

– turned always leftward
to see without disfigurement
your spirit dancing on the lawn
– now drifting nowhere
in storm and sea wrack
with my last ship gone down

PICTURES ON TELEVISION

– for Pat Lane

Refugees on the roads
of countries across the world
plodding the highways
from somewhere to nowhere
– the woman seen behind a glass screen
dressed in a shapeless dress
dragging a tired child by the hand
you could not know she is pregnant
and dreaming of the new child
– or the man with face pitted by smallpox
dreaming about what death is like
you could not know

Their expressions beyond the glass
are nearly the same
human vivacity and sparkle
assuming they possessed such qualities
have become abstractions
unreal to themselves
– one man's jaws move silently
he talks to someone inside himself
who answers reassuringly
that the long journey will end soon
in warmth and comfort and love
the man tells himself he believes
that other person inside
and both of them are lying

You watch them in the living room
their faces reflect here and there

on end tables and nearby windows
sisters and brothers and aunts and cousins
the gamut of relationships
sometimes lovers
fenced off by the glass screen
but whether lovers can endure
such intimate knowledge of each other
or think anything important but themselves
is an interesting question
– and when there's a knock at your own door
you feel like saying "Be right back"
and leave them to answer it

Dreaming is living backwards:
in the mind's reverse gear
I ride the same freight trains
I rode long ago in Saskatchewan:

Saskatchewan –
the name produces ripples in the mind
travelling through a lost childhood
and ride those crooning syllables
to where all dreams begin
and climb the sky-steps to Alberta
and B.C. mountains like stone seeds
sprout alpine flowers
inside my neolithic skull
they jam into the bedroom
I squash them flat
and spread them out
to make a mountain blanket
I wrap around the world

Ontario is trees
the kind that meet from both
sides of the road
and make a continual whisper
and nothing begins or ends
but cities are aberration
do not exist in my mind
are green mirage in the land-sea
in which people drift by
and forget where they were going
Quebec is a long grey sidewalk

going nowhere and people cry out
where is nowhere?
and I don't know what to tell them
In the Maritimes .
all those provinces heave and lift
as if there were land-tides
where a girl swims up to me
and demands a fish
I tell her I don't have a fish
sorry
would a jackhammer do?
but I don't have one of those either
and we weep for jackhammers

Back among the crooning syllables
Saskatchewan
the name becomes
quadruplet sisters .
I ask them all to marry me
just so their name can mingle with mine
forever and forever yesterday
and Alberta you marry me too
and we'll forget your maternal parent
and live in geographic polygamy
Manitoba you are stern and silent
which is just as well
your winters are spirit-glaciers
Portage & Main is an Ice Age
with a white blossom of frost
decorating the sun's face

On the Pacific I have kidnapped an island
from a rich dog-salmon
and take it home with me

park it beside the bed
and now I dream of islands
in a spring of wild roses
and write another poem
in this enchanted country

NAKED WITH SUMMER IN YOUR MOUTH

Riding the mountain ridges
where the avalanche waits in winter
to spill its full moon torrents
onto the trembling ski trails –

But summer
perched atop the boxcars
hugging myself in morning cold
then drinking the sun's white whiskey
and beginning to realize
there is no past and no future
you're born at this precise moment
in the high mountains
the roots have climbed your summit

Well – that's all very dramatic
I hear someone say to myself
and it's me saying it:
a very long time later
the margins and edges of time
and place have widened for me
euphoria in the blood stream
yeast in the gluteus maximus
and an obvious senility
send me back into summer
climbing the switchback highways
reversing again into winter
in Arcturus and the Pleiades
Orion and his dog in the sky
where time has lost its boundaries
and space jumpstarts to infinity

I return to the mountains
my roots have climbed your summit

CHAC MOOL AT CHICHEN ITZA

Five hundred years of sun and rain
have pounded Yucatan limestone
to dust then back to stone again
– I am a stranger here to this god
with the broken face
and scarcely worthy of his notice
where he lies with sacrificial bowl
extended before him
and manages a recumbent arrogance

A country the colour of an old brown dog
where men have gone mad staring
at a sky clamped down on their heads
or remained so terribly sane
they mocked at heathen gods

I sit at the pool's edge
a sweating tourist
where priests sacrificed to the sun
the same sun as this morning
                    the same water
and I wait for the resplendent quetzal bird
– he comes when my mind is empty of things
and the jungle silent
the bird a scarcely believable rainbow
a sunset with wings
posing for its own photograph
then gone
and an old brown dog wanders by in the dust

Slowly back on a stone pathway
winding around the pyramids
the sky darkens to grey
and the grey god in his temple waits
the god with a broken face
his head turned sideways to look at me
his head with holes for eyes:
You who refuse to believe in gods
shall find nothing else to believe in –

WOMAN

– and some whose home is the wind
that lifts the curtains at night
when you wake up and don't know why
and she is there too and unprovable
as the sun on the other side of the world

– and now there is only myself here
in this cage of bones kept prisoner
forever and cannot be free
to hover and hover as a moth
hovers around its beloved light
beloved light

GUARD DUTY

Standing guard at a crashed one-engine
Fairey Battle fighter-bomber in 1940:

the plane went down so hard
its engine plunged deep in earth
the fuselage remaining above ground
torn and ragged from falling down the sky
I thought of the boy as young as me
in his cockpit up there
with lots of time to know what was happening
and wondering how to use the last few
moments of his life and maybe not
being able to remember that girl's name
on the Toronto train three years ago
before it stopped mattering
and whether there was time to scratch
an itch and watch the earth and trees
coming up fast
in a reversal of being born
– and there's a moment when you'd know
what it's really like
to be dead

THE POOR BASTARD

An interior landscape
— a seascape really
in which an exhausted oarsman
is rowing a dinghy through barrier reefs
toward a calm sunlit lagoon
beyond which is a tropical island

— this landscape inside my head
has no other boundaries
sometimes weather there is stormy
with lightning splitting dark clouds
sometimes moonlight or just ordinary weather
and this scene is always there
no matter what time I look inward
lying in bed waiting for sleep
or waking up in the morning
and doing the small everyday things
one does in the course of a lifetime

I look inward and there he is
wearing a torn shirt and ragged trousers
with broken blisters on his hands
struggling to get through that reef
twisting the boat sideways round fangs of rock
undersea currents grabbing at him
— everything seems quite ordinary
except that it takes place inside my head
except that it seems a matter of life and death
a man struggling to row a small boat
inside a safe sunlit lagoon
— once the man watching elsewhere

saw oars strike dark blue water
to a dazzle of sunlit commotion
and yelled hoarsely

How long all this has been going on
is impossible for me to determine
but I suspect the oarsman has been there
for as long as I can remember
the extraordinary aspects of the situation
now blunted by time and taken for granted
– the weather inside is always variable
the oarsman himself often discouraged
I've seen him with shoulders bent over
head down and arms hung loosely
soaked to the skin with rain
or head and back crusted with snow
– at other times he works fiercely
the set of his jaw rigid as metal
face always turned away from me
nevertheless it seems I know him
the angle of his shoulders familiar
I'm plagued with this half-recognition
some vital aspect always missing
something that would solve this puzzle

Everybody does this I suppose
sees friends' faces in their minds
and conjures up scenes from the past
lost loves and times of great elation
but the difference here: a permanent landscape
that's always there when I look inward
I could even draw a map of the place
seen from a great distance
like a moon-map inside my head

Sometimes I am impatient with the oarsman
and say to him "Why don't you give up
ship the oars and just drift away
wherever the wind and tides take you . . ."
At other times I feel sympathy for him
and whisper under my breath "Go ahead
Don't let a few rocks stop you . . ."
On the other hand I wonder about that lagoon
always changing and always the same
is it worthwhile to make all this effort
and grow old working for nothing tangible
unless it's just survival
but I don't know the answer to that

Again I watch the struggling oarsman
seeing his shoulders droop head sink down
as if he'd been listening to my thoughts
and decided the lagoon isn't worth it
noticing the blood on his hands
bruises on his bare arms
as a whirlpool spins the boat round
and round almost out of control
But I leave him there alone
there's really nothing I can do for him
except look in from time to time
and after a while I wonder again
what use it is – this looking inward
and my friend (I say now he's my friend) .
who has never seen my face
as I've never seen his in its entirety
which is perhaps the reason I give myself
for continuing to watch the poor bastard
I want to see his face
and tonight before sleep look inward again

and notice a storm is making in the west
and urge him to make a final effort
also notice with dismay
the dinghy has sprung a leak
the oarsman is forced to bail frantically
in fact the boat may even be sinking
– but I must stop this stupid prying
into someone else's life
and get to sleep

IN THE DESERT

– for Milton Acorn

My friends die off one by one:
and far away in the desert
caravans are plodding thru the sand
I can see them at the horizon's edge
the young on their many roads to Mecca
but I have been there often
and returned again

My friends die off:
far distant in waste places
the living move in many directions
I could run after them shouting
across the desert "Wait for me –"
And sometimes I have done that
but things went badly for me
and rushing to meet those people
excited and panting
their faces change into someone else
their faces change . . .

This morning
wandering the grey desert
looking for a cactus flower
in the wrong season
with caravans moving in the distance
sinking under grey horizons
I noticed someone moving in the shadows
coming toward me at a great pace
and they cried out as I had done
"Wait for me –"

A single figure
and impossible to say
whether male or female
crossing the sand dunes shouting
arriving where I stand waiting
in a great flurry of dust and sand:
it was someone I did not know
and very young
I was about to say in a neutral voice
"You had better go back –"

But looking into that eager face
and hopeful eyes –: I glimpsed the flux
of what exists and does not yet exist
a wavering between disappointment and joy
and knew there was only a moment left
before the little gap in time healed itself
I said welcome
and knew this messenger from the desert
was someone I had been waiting for
and clasped them in my arms
the stranger

RETURN JOURNEY

Red leaves
in deep woods of October
red leaves winging
through the air
are coloured birds
are kites
are souls of trees
are someone else's poem
– mine too

In towns of northern counties
towns set deep in forests
I've returned to adolescence
childlike and nearly carefree
and kicked householders' piles of
leaves into nearby gutters
for no reason or any
– maybe a juvenile delight
in watching red leaves dancing
In Trenton and Belleville
I've acted more circumspectly
– they know me there?
or else the sombre oak trees
              orange-brown and dull gold
are sobering
alas as I grow older
are sobering for me

I've seen such autumns in my life!
– a thousand thousand red-haired girls
whose morning ice at last gives way

in afternoon to maple fire
and warm the earth with love
(I can't believe
in all the tropic lands
I've visited in other years
I can't believe
those countries have any equivalent
to our autumn changelings
or tint the midnight crimson
and dream in colour
the way my country does)
One time when Cabbagetown streets
were covered deep with leaves
I rushed about like a ten-year-old
arms linked with a friend
and both of us were ten-year-olds
we kicked the leaves in unison
then rushed off laughing
to gather armloads
and stuff them down
each other's collars
– well I was sixty then
and that is hard for me to believe

I spent my early years
yearning to be grown-up
and now spend nearly as much time
reverting to childhood
and this year I plan another
trip to those northern places
alone this time
to stand in that great welter of colour
orange umber salmon lemon crimson bronze gold
until the mind refuses to handle

all the glory it can't get used to
and yet cannot do without
and I've finally changed places
with whoever I was then
whoever I am now
a child listening
to the land's poem

EARLE BIRNEY IN HOSPITAL

He knows me and does not
know me and the fatal
facility for transposing
myself into another someone
ends with me peering out
from his eyes into my eyes
and dizzily thinking
My God! My God!
I have stopped being Me!

But calmer now:
he knows me and does not
know me and I am a coloured
shadow in sunlight
his brow furrowed and puzzled
with the effort of not knowing
poems he's written and not written
yet that will never be
and he smiles in memory
what might be memory
of whatever smiling was
and it is somehow left for me
to write them remembering pain
of not writing beyond
this grey land of nowhere
forgetting the pain before
beautiful verb and handsome noun
agreed to live together
for better or worse somehow
and kicked their heels
in the printed word

while the shadow stranger waits
the strange shadow
watching and ill at ease
and a little afraid:

as he questions himself
asks himself: *Who is this guy?*
Why is he here?

At that very moment
when the puzzlement is greatest
I smile at him
and the *why* and the smile together
glow just beyond the poem
and shine on his face and his face shines
and for that one moment
my friend remembers
among the multiple choices
of his lost remembering
he chooses
and the poem blossoms

Ol Ez: – the man who knew everything
– after *A Lume Spento* his first book
that echoed every other writer
he advised Yeats advised Eliot
on how to write their poems
and sentenced the world to purgatory
for not listening to him except
on Italian Fascist radio in wartime:
"The 60 kikes who started this war
might be sent to St. Helena"
                and
"Roosevelt is more in the hands
of the Jews than Wilson was in 1919"
– and after they locked him up
in a steel cage at Pisa in boiling
sun for months and after sixteen
years locked up in St. Elizabeth's
Hospital as a madman
                remember him
finding an ancient Chinese poet
and recreating another man's verse:
"Two small people, without dislike
or suspicion" in the village of Chokan
thirteen hundred years ago
arriving instantly in your mind
without detours and whispering
to you from behind the west wind:
"At fifteen I stopped scowling
I desired my dust to be mingled with yours
For ever and for ever and for ever –"

We humans: there is no explaining us
our cruelty and nastiness and nobility
and all you can do now is read
"The River Merchant's Wife"
and say "Pound"
                    and shrug your shoulders

To his sister when Swinburne died in 1909:
"Now I am the King of the Cats"

What does one say of a man
who believed in fairies
– and swooned metrically all his life
for a strident female patriot
– who was accused of being Fascist
with perhaps some reason
– and subscribed to the beliefs of Madame Blavatsky
whose name might be spelled "charlatan"
– and in old age contemplated
an operation to restore sexual vigour
– what does one say?

– at a conservative estimate
fifty thousand people
in a dozen different countries
          all over the world
will stop whatever they're doing
several times a year
and a thought wrapped up
in a few commonplace words
will sing in their minds like summer
– for them the sound of traffic ends
a man will pull his car off the road
and sit there motionless
a woman with a wet dinner plate in her hand
will stand there holding onto it
in the sudden silence of her mind
while the sun and the sky and the clouds

and the sea
are quivering in otherwhere
and time does not look back
at the man beside the road
or the woman washing dishes
for whom nothing is important
but something they can't describe
or even talk about
except to quote another man's words
that moment in your lifetime
when the body and mind
have joined themselves to another mind
– and there is an improbable glimmer
of fairies in the twilight
and patriotism seems very necessary
and mysticism quite feasible
and sexual vigour admirable
and silence
thunders into a continuing silence

Frost boasting at Amherst
about springing Pound from the loony bin:
"Archie couldn't do it!
Hemingway couldn't do it!
Williams couldn't do it!"
— especially proud of that because
he disliked Pound and felt noble
about going to Eisenhower's Attorney
General Herbert Brownell
and managing to sublimate his dislike

He said once that "Free
verse is like playing tennis
without a net" — table tennis anyone?
— a man to admire but not love
dangerous either way
and crazy for adulation.
It's the anthology pieces that get you:
"Stopping by Woods —" "Desert Places" and
"Never Again Would Birds' Song Be the Same"
— well Shapiro says "No passion"
but I think very strong feeling
and isn't that passion?
— a kind of madness underneath
all that homespun philosophy
a son's suicide and a daughter's hatred
adding up to a very strange poet

But quite often he sounds exactly
like my old Sunday-school teacher
and there's something about "Good

fences make good neighbours" turns
immediately into a cliché
and so do many other lines:
— grownups want to learn
and not be taught — and saying that
you see exactly what I mean

However: you can't dislike him
by pleading major differences from yourself
you might've disguised things better
the snake and centipede crawling
out of your head unobserved
Poems that presume a soul
and drip honey where yours might be
poems that shrivel the scrotum
or vagina and watch you
in your own mirror changing
into someone you do not recognize

And you think of him
— a man leaving a warm house at night
late at night and wandering alone
looking out from beneath a bridge
at the wandering stars
and nothingness surrounding them
and hear the whisper of his mind working:
Would it be possible
could the stars' glory be sublimated
by a poem?
— and will there be time?

Musing: that a man (or woman) is
surrounded by nothingness is undeniable
the nature of things is nothingness

– and he must people that space
all around him by himself
and the kind of person
he has become in a lifetime:

unfocus your eyes then
– the tenants of darkness
shadowy on the periphery
before you finally let go of things –

Lake water sings into ice
– the mysterious everyday stuff
you can drink or drown in
can't be depended on and
now is changing before my eyes

I shine my flashlight along
this shoreline searching for
the moment the exact instant
of hey-presto creation
– and the materia medica of chemistry
whereby the process is possible
and physics of matter and energy
mean nothing before my intense curiosity
that shuts out everything else
– hurting my knees on sharp rocks
peering into dark changing water
wanting to feel as water feels
as the werewolf feels
in its last human moment
nothing large or dramatic
just this hangnail curiosity
while my mind empties itself
and the instant wavers
and the lake blossoms
a silver rose of pure sound

my flashlight picks them out
the new-born baby ice cubes
tiny jellyfish jostling together
for cold comfort

their hydrogen-oxygen mother
penetrated by a dark stranger

I kneel on the rocks and shiver
designated oddball to my neighbours
once again being ridiculous
and thereby cut off from any company
but the loon crying in darkness
and dead writers in silent books
the woman waiting in a warm house
who does not know she is waiting
while ice sings its small music
and the cold comes
from far away on Baffin and Ellesmere
glaciers inch perceptibly closer
and I'm not dressed for this
blood-sugar low
(whatever that means)
and now I'm overwhelmed by sadness
anticlimax
post-parturition and coitus
interruptus blues
detumescence of curiosity

Dissatisfied with myself
I wander back to the house
peer out the kitchen window
remembering the birth-cry of ice
while the world behind glass
is changing into winter

FLIGHT OF THE ATLANTIS

At Cape Canaveral the spaceship
rises on a diarrhoea of fire
explosions rock the earth
the earth mantle shudders
dishes and cutlery gyrate on shelves
old bones in graves dance
outside a strange daylight holds
each leaf flower blade of grass
stands in shimmering detachment
and achieve their most-possible selves

At sea
the dark components of light
and silent components of sound
weave ghostly murals in the sky
on land
armadillos stop in their tracks
suddenly naked
with all the planets staring at them
– rattlesnake jaws fall open
stars glitter on their fangs
– pelicans – the grey costume jewellery
of earth – wait for taxidermists
and continue their dream of serenity

Cities principalities powers –
we have forgotten
whatever is important
except "marvellous" science
clichés abounding
we recede backwards from womb to womb

in the flash photography of eternity
at least relinquishing everything
at most only remembering
the sound of summer voices

SELF-PORTRAIT

A face in the mirror, an imitation of me:
you can't ever see your real face,
only this silvery cartoon grinning
like a clown, posturing for an audience
which is yourself. Just my body is real
for me, and then only half of it
– the rest behind me like a rumour.

My face,
ordinary enough to be remarkable
body like an awkward child,
eyes washed-out bluish-greenish,
rear-view mirrors.

That face,
washed up on ancient beaches,
a hundred generations on will be
so watered down, divided and subdivided
the tiny fragment left of me unrecognizable,
but reaching reaching
– splinter of flesh, droplet of memory,
searching searching
for one familiar thing, turning on itself,
a muscular spasm in someone else's face,
a twitch, stammering into nothing.

Revisit the splinter of me,
someone uneasily examines the mirror,
glimpsing that other peering at him:
my poor friend, my lost inheritor,

I have much sympathy for you,
the man in the mirror
who screams and keeps on screaming,
and does not know why . . .

1.
Meeting her again was like a series
of atonements for something
he couldn't remember –

2.
Only when my mother
          dead for forty years
my father three-quarters of a century
have receded as if they never were
did it occur to me to tell them
about the loon I saw this morning
flying over the lake
as if they could enjoy the sight now
as much as when they were alive

3.
– I grow old
and walk along the lakeshore
to watch the small fish
dart away from the land-monster

Returning to the house
I remember those others
my lost ones
friends that faded loves that cooled
the mind-pain of losing someone
and having to become another
person from who you thought you were
– a small amphibian emerging
from the water whispers breathlessly

"How does it feel?
How does it feel?"

It feels like death

4.
And a few enemies
– do I forgive them?
Of course not
they demonstrate conclusively
Planck's "Third Law of Thermodynamics"
about brainless falling apples
(or was that Isaac Newton?)
and besides
I don't want to lose them
my enemies
I enjoy their company
at funerals

THE BOOBY HOP

The female bird dances
on a stone stage
covered with dried
booby shit left
foot right foot
et cetera vice versa
to show off
those marvellous blue feet
no shoe may encumber
on this island shrine
for a pedomorphic god

Two land iguanas
with fallen jaws
in terpsichorean wonder
are also spectators
in front-row seats
on freebies of course
and from the parrot
snout of one a
trickle of saliva
which I think indicates
appreciation
or a head cold

(A bifurcated creature
minus feathers
may also be included
among those present
but ignored to the degree
of complete invisibility

which might be taken
as a booby compliment?)

Now the male booby
whistles loudly
and otherwise demonstrates
masculine approval
as males are wont to do
in like circumstances
and spreads his wings
denoting adoration
After the dance sequence
they select dry grass
choose bits of twigs
to play house with
in short they
demonstrate conclusively
what they have in mind
There is then a presentation
with some formality
grass and twigs are exchanged
and each bows low
as if to say
with Wendell Holmes
"Build thee more stately
mansions O my soul –"
– and it strikes me forcibly
that I have seen something very
similar to all this before
in Westmount and Rosedale

Galapagos Islands

the exact moment
not the incident or entire happening
a shapeless bulk in the mind
but the instant
the needle's point
when time divides
into before and after
leaving behind
a clown's face
at the beginning of things:

When she leaned forward
I could see the white ghosts of breasts
shape themselves to reality
an inclination of my head
and a pink nipple like a wild raspberry
melted in my mouth
– and she turned toward me
caught my eye
and knew

I had stolen a handful of silver
from my grandfather's coin hoard
while he was in the john
returning he said
"How much did you steal"
voice stripped of anything
his face hung there in sepia light
of 1924
while I groped for love

In the mind's eye
seeing myself dead
collapsed on the kitchen floor
peering upward sightlessly
expression indicating curiosity
as if the mind was continuing active
speculating
about the reception elsewhere
– but I've failed
and realize now
escape is nearly impossible

When the phone said "Tom is dead"
and I yelled NO
at the mouthpiece
the moment folded and repeated itself
possessed duration
and became pain
the world blanked out
I was alone
watching the expanding universe
a white scarf of the Milky Way
flung round creation
and a moment later
the sense of nothingness
so overpowering reality wavered
in a world of
diminished certainties

The woman standing naked beside a bed
telephoning
pulling back from light in the doorway
almost as if she was recoiling from
Phidias' chisel on the Athenian Acropolis

if it wasn't for that telephone
– so enchanting in her hinterlands
as the dimples undulate

a fox a fox a red fox
running in front of my headlights
near the farm in Little Ireland
his tail a red hot poker
streamed in the wind of his passage
– and it seemed like this was forever
we had been running together forever
at least from Monday to Friday
and I was a child in a story
and he was the friend I included
we were both on our way to nowhere
in a dream from my long ago childhood
when I was pursued by bad men
or wolf wolf wolf
– then I slowed and he vanished forever
and ran to include me in his story
for his friends to listen and marvel
how he was pursued by a monster
and I wonder I wonder
               do foxes dream?

Riding a bicycle into the country
with another kid named Bernard Campbell
when I was 12 or 13 years old:
seeing a woman come racing out of
a miserable shack made of bits
and pieces of scrap lumber
she trying to climb a wire fence
before a man wearing overalls caught
her and started to beat her to death

the woman screaming and screaming
and the sound of that scream
slicing off bits and pieces
of my youth moment by moment until
I stand at the bathroom mirror
watching a shapeless gasping face
that tries to escape being human
a monkey that doesn't want to be either

OH GOD OH CHARLOTTETOWN

My most cherished memory
of the potato city:
walking the main drag
toward the beer store
excited by soaring skyscrapers
I spot this modest brick building
surmounted by a three-foot bust
probably marble and quite dirty
since it dates to around 1900
I am curious
and ask about it at a stationery
store across the road:
it seems the guy
who owned this brick building
had his own image carved up there
his name sounded like Taylor
There could only be one reason
for that sculpture
Taylor wanted fame
and that was his immortality
perched up there in sun and rain
flesh changed to stone
stone that yearns to be human
stone that just yearns
forever
– at least until a dirty virus
grabs the Great Lord Spud
or the ghost of Milton Acorn
walks at midnight
and will not stop talking

Remember Herostratus
in 356 B.C.?
– the guy that burned
down the Temple of Diana
one of the Seven Wonders
of the World in ancient Ephesus
the site often pointed
out by local con men to tourists
while lifting their wallets
Herostratus was not shy
about his incendiary reasons
"I wanna be famous
          I wanna I wanna –"
he was often heard to say
to visiting firemen
before parishioners of the goddess
Diana chased his tail outa town

Later in Ameliasburgh
I am cogitating about Charlottetown
wondering who will be remembered
there after half a century
Milton Acorn   Herostratus   Taylor
or the Great God Spud?
I'd prefer it to be Acorn
but deep in the red earth
of his home island
I doubt if he cares much

AGES

I am four years old
the most important person
ever born on earth
— life bursts into flame
for me the night stars shine
for me it's always June
days are bright discoveries
in my infinite bedroom world
the moon's a silver spoon

I am very young
only 16
I will never die
the years are made
of edible gold braid
the weeks are sun sun
and endless endless
the days stand still

I am 25 now
and feel the same
only more so
the world's a lovely place
full of birds' cries
and all my own
the birds like little jewels
belong to me

I am 32
and know a lady here
on this lovely earth

each day she steps out of
the sunrise glow
emerging like a star
I walk my life with her

I am 40 now
and knowing less and less
each day I live
bewildered by the loss
of gifts existence gives
still foolish but finally
I've learned how
to curse what I can't bless

Now I grumble aloud
and scream my discontent
BUT GOD HOW LUCKY I WAS
for all the friends I had
for the look in a woman's eyes
for the death I refuse to die
and scream my lust and rage
to the God I don't believe in
to god and all the gods
plural and singular
but god does not reply

HEROES

The mirror is broken
(glass is fragile anyway)
Jason Odysseus Hector
and beautiful Pallas Athene
                 all heroes die
– replaced by a man named Sakharov
and a couple of writers
who don't look like much
let alone heroes
Václav Havel maybe
and nothing is lost
I am enriched beyond measure
by the living and some who died
before me
           Ol Rid for one
he looked something like a pine tree
with all its needles shaved off
my grandfather
who spent some time on Olympos himself
and took no shit from the gods

In October when I'm driving
among the windy townships
of high hill country
Herschel Monteagle Dungannon
all the red leaves falling
are a royal flush
of either hearts or diamonds
I hear a chuckle
in the relay sub-station
at Ol Rid's poker table

where someone
must've dropped a bundle
and I return south
to play my hand

STAN ROGERS

In the smoke and fire
at Cincinnati
Stan Rogers dancing
the tall man in all of us
when Air Canada
(Flight No. 797)
touched down on the airport runway
with a fire in the rear toilet
survivors say
– but Stan did not survive

In the smoke at Cincinnati
he is not there
but "driving hard across the plains"
for the Northwest Passage
my friend
whom I never knew
whose spirit haunts me
a man not like any of us
and yet exactly the same

What do you say about friendship
about a friend
in our punctured lifetimes
when all of us live so briefly?
– you deny that
deny the little measurers
and counters of unimportant things
you scream at the calendar
and spit in the face of time
you say We live forever

and sometimes longer
– then you fall asleep
as we all do

But there he is
Stan Rogers
"driving hard across the plains"
and "the mileage clicking west"
longer than forever
far from Cincinnati
the tall man in all of us
dreaming of a country
dreaming of home

I am dive-bombed by swallows
nesting in our garage
and all my assurances of goodwill
have no effect whatever
– and their lovely swooping flight
sun tangled in bodies
breast dull orange
bearing down on my head
like bullets with tail feathers
is not very reassuring
Still it does occur to me
that one of them might be Procne
who once picked the wrong husband
and now lives in our cold country
yearning for Athens
and the Isles of Greece

Itys into Goldfinch

Procne's son in our front yard?
– looping-the-loop at Roblin lake
going "yip yip" like a cowboy
dressed all in yellow
riding an invisible bronco
In the unlikely event
that heaven actually does exist
the goldfinch must be there
homesick for earth

I wake up dammit at six and five
and four a.m. all spring and summer
the noisy birds haunt my sleep
lecture me about early rising
expound the benefits of foreign travel
and how tourism sublimates sex:

Robin just back from Guatemala
                    and the Indies
goes "cheerily-cheerily"
in my cedars and wants to know
what's new in Canada?
Oriole from Colombia and Mexico
whistles romantically "truly-truly"
like he's proposing or something
and I hope the lady refused him
Bobolink home from the Amazon
strums his banjo at Ameliasburgh
and his mate cusses humans
("Damn that plate glass window!"
– nearly whapped herself last week
when she saw her own spittin image
flying toward her singing and
wants those people to post warnings)
Now the mourning dove
          goes "oh-Woe-Woe-WOE"
with which sentiments I heartily agree
since I can't sleep any more
– then unexpectedly sleep comes
I sleep and dream again
dream ahead to autumn

and wake in winter
of my old age whispering
to the little wanderers
    "Oh take me with you
        wherever you're going –"

There is Margaret Atwood
– she is meeting Premier Peterson
in the Ontario Legislative Buildings
he is congratulating her
for being Margaret Atwood

There is Margaret Atwood
– she is swinging a champagne bottle
against the bow of a super icebreaker
it winces noticeably from the blow
and escapes into the water
muttering
"My name is Henry Larson"

There is Margaret Atwood
– she is accepting the Nobel Prize
and reporters are crowding around
with tears in their eyes
asking why she is so marvellous
she replies simply and modestly
"I am Margaret Atwood"

There is Margaret Atwood
– sitting in an unmanned spaceship
waiting for blast-off her lovely
eyes slightly dilated from a sleeping
drug administered by flight surgeons
She wakes at the edge of the universe
where someone says "Hello
Pleased to meet you Ms. Atwood
My name is God" She smiles

and writes the name down promptly
in her little notebook to prevent
forgetfulness

There is Margaret Atwood
– at the edge of the universe
speaking to the First Cause at last
he is slightly ill at ease and says
"Did you have a nice trip"
"Reasonably so – and I'm glad to see
there are no autograph hunters around
(he had been about to ask for hers)
But where do we go from here?"

Beyond the solemn hinterlands of nothingness
beyond the last lonesome uninhabited galaxy
("There are rooms for rent in the outer planets" –
                                   Travel Brochure)
in the calm green meadowlands of heaven
being interviewed by the neutered blessed seraphim
concerning the relative importance of YIN and yang
– there is Margaret Atwood

PROCNE INTO ROBIN

To dance like that in firelight
with music playing
and throw off all your clothes
around midnight
is no ordinary woman's way
with a man and no
you are no ordinary
woman but a bird
I have just made this discovery
– not the Greek bird Procne
                nor her sister Philomela
not swallow or nightingale
as the gods changed them to –
not exactly your namesake either
for she is much too red-breasted
and you're white all over or nearly
I have made another discovery
those short dainty steps of yours
are the shore-birds dance steps
on a storm-battered beach
after the rough waves recede
stitching the world back together
And when you hover over me
I am already at your feet
unable to say anything
only murmur as men do
and wait
when they know the little dancer
from the sky must rest sometimes
must rest soon
with folded wings
and wait

ARCHILOCHUS IN THE DEMOTIC

– for Sam Solecki

First poet of the Western World
of whose work we possess fragments only
and those on accounta this bunch of academics
in ancient Egypt quoted his stuff
in their own writings
                                    and later on embalmers
shoved the profs' wastepaper-papyri
into the bosoms of mummies for packing
along with the Papyrus of Ani which
supplied passwords for the Land of the Dead
to bigshot Egyptians

One can easily imagine
some dead Pharaoh or other
reaching for Ani's handy guidebook
for the right hieratic passwords
and came up with Archie instead:

Lykambes on Paros Island
denies his daughter to Rameses
(as he once had to Archie)
and the much-insulted Pharaoh
summons Anubis the jackal-headed god
and patron of embalmers in the Underworld
to chastise Lykambes in demotic Egyptian
at which point Zeus and Athena happen by
and give Anubis what-for in Mycenaean Greek

and there's Archie's lost shield lying around
now belonging to a buck-toothed Thracian tribesman

while Pindar and Simonides look down their noses
and sneer at Archie in Linear B
for comparing Greek and Egyptian mythologies
and mistaking embalming fluid for cantharides
while Homer across the Aegean in Asia
raises up on one elbow complaining
"Shaddup and leave me sleep"
– which is how Archie got enrolled at Oxford
under a phony name and wrote
"Horseman Pass By" on Pergamum vellum
(revised by Ezra P. and Margaret A.)
– and all on accounta some Egyptian profs
iambic trimeter and trochaic tetrameter are
quoted by truckdrivers

And Lykambes' daughter on Paros Island
switched her ass sexily and said
"Okay" to Rameses before the old man
could stop her and Archie
in the midst of his heartbreak
– he just wrote another poem

it was all very confusing

Beside the cold snow-fed Isar River –
carved by a Bavarian peasant
Christ as a man of middle age
a farmer
and a sturdiness about him
"with some of the meanness of the peasant,
but also with a kind of dogged nobility –"
rudimentary face staring up at the mountains
lighted with white radiance of alpine snow
neck rigid, resisting nails and cross
pinned down but stubborn
rejecting this public disgrace
and white light from the mountains
streaming down
across the old imperial road

Closer to Austria in a glass case
– the river vanishing
inside a forest
with a hoarse cry
– a small meditating Christ
wearing a peasant cloak of red flannel
mind full of questions
about his own death
wearing "a little crown of thorns"

In Austria itself –
the sculptor perhaps a professional
– an artist from Vienna?
his carving larger than life-size
portraying a dead Christus

artistically
shortly after the crucifixion
body hanging forward on the nails
as if being alive any longer
was completely hopeless
– beside the silent mountains
and noisy river
Death but lately absent

Turning south –
"One Christus is very elegant,
combed and brushed and foppish on his cross"
other Christs
"turn up their faces and roll
back their eyes very piteously"
"others again are beautiful as elegies"

In a valley near St. Jakob
Christ is a big powerful man
sitting there beside the grave
not long after the Resurrection
weakness very apparent
but mixed with seething hatred
– for whom?

Close to Meran
a fallen Christus
probably by a local craftsman
the Son of God
flat on his back
limbs wedge-shaped and elemental
arms broken off at the shoulders
hanging loosely from their nails
wind moving them back and forth

as if they were alive
as if they were still alive

*

And it is a strange feeling for me
beside Roblin Lake near Ameliasburgh
to be talking about Jesus as the Son of God
as if he were divine
and I struggling to be human –

Photo of Gabrielle Roy with her much-lived-
in face a relief map with all the wrinkles
like badges of honour
her face a banner in the wind
Two of Margaret Laurence whom I loved dearly
one looking bored the other alight with amusement
Don Coles' poem which says so much about the
lost "Forests of the Medieval World" it loses
me in places I've never been
Harold Ballard on the cover of *Saturday Night*
his cane spanking the world in geriatric rage
My sister-in-law at age twenty-two
so beautiful the photo sizzles despairingly
knowing this one chance was lost
Acorn of course
who dreamed himself into otherwhere
and never found his way home
Me pissing behind the Owen Roblin tombstone
only the stream of piss visible in photo
presaging dry centuries
Poster of Atwood's breasts surmounted by
her Proteus-face which she objected to
or would cancel the reading
Tiff Findley's verse from Euripides
which says "never that which is shall die"
pollyanna stuff but I like it
Eurithe as a fifty-year-old child in water-
colour pretending she isn't there
but she always has been
Xerox of Milosz with cigar looking cynical
Gary Snyder poet-smug and Wm. Everson a dead prophet

Ben Johnson beating Carl Lewis in Rome
grinning back at him like a little boy
saying "Haw-Haw-Haw" without stopping
MacLeish's "You, Andrew Marvell"
– and I too follow shadows around the world
at Petra and Ecbatan and Sumer and Palmyra
and sleep in those ruined cities still
Two original Lawrence letters
both so alive he can't be dead
Three Kipling poems I like much
megaphones into silence
Colour photo: on rock slopes of Nimrud Dag
in Turkey: wrecked stone heads of kings
whose makers placed this glory
atop the mountain
I sit in my rotating office chair and marvel
and wonder that thought itself
could body forth such shapes and forms

I have gathered them all together
like a casual group of strangers
at this meeting place under my roof
who will never meet again
their only relationship supplied by me
who told them to come here
to wait and be silent on my wall
while I contemplate
not their nature but my own
and know as much about myself
by proxy as from looking deep
into the mirror of what I am

It is very puzzling
this flow of self outward

and silent reception in return
and being pinned to a wall
and being what passes for human
and looking again outward
to see myself
a shadow in the sunlight

INCIDENT INVOLVING WILLIAM BLAKE

– at Felpham, Sussex, 1803

I am at present in a bustle to defend myself
against a very unwarrantable warrant
from a Justice of the Peace in Chichester,
which was taken out against me by a private
in Captain Leathes' troop of 1st or Royal
Dragoons, for an assault and seditious words.
His Enmity arises from my having turned him
out of my Garden, into which he was invited
as an assistant by a Gardener at work therein,
without my knowledge. I desired him, as politely
as possible, to go out of the Garden;
he made me an impertinent answer.
He then threaten'd to knock out my Eyes,
with many foolish imprecations
& with some contempt for my person.
I therefore took him by the Elbows
& pushed him before me till I had got him out;
there I intended to have left him,
but he, turning about, put himself
into a Posture of Defiance, threatening
& swearing at me. I, perhaps foolishly
& perhaps not, stepped out at the Gate,
& putting aside his blows, took him again
by the Elbows, & keeping his back to me,
pushed him forwards down the road about fifty yards –
he all the time endeavouring to turn around
& strike me, & raging & cursing, when I
had got him to where he was Quarter'd,
which was very quickly done –

BROTHER

– the one who was given no name
                and died before me
whom I cannot refer to at all
except through the relationship
almost "like aunts or pets or foreigners"
but not a foreigner
some part of myself
I'm trying to find again

Lost in bewilderment
I pray to whatever gods there be
any of the old ones
Osiris or what-have-you
who happened to survive
hanging around on street-corners
begging for credence
or enough money for booze
I pray to Odin Zeus Yahweh Athena
            Quetzalcoatl any of them
                Destroy my certainties
                    Give me something to believe in
                        For I am a fool

There is no one but myself:
rivers flushing the continents
mountains that have no name
flowers that are only flowers
seas crowded with fish
the land with strangers
and my own voice speaks to me
            Who shall I love?

and inside me a schoolmasterish voice
                corrects my grammar

– the brother who was given no name
                for he died too soon
relinquished the rivers and mountains
scarcely aware they existed
forsook the taste and scent of earth
renounced the love of women
and chose the dust
and chose to feel nothing more

– the brother who was given no name
he was like the wind
here for a day or a moment
coming and going in instant summer
with no name except the remembering
– as the flower is only a flower
but a biological necessity
for the plant's survival
as he was for me
Brother
        I say to him
                Brother

Later on
among the shadows
I will not be a stranger

GARY: SELF-PORTRAIT

I still have it at Ameliasburgh
the painting he discarded as a failure
and project it on the mind-screen:
dark hair growing low on his forehead
skin the colour of old ivory
slender aristocratic nose
and an extremely snooty look
with which he viewed himself
as if he were intruding without
permission on his own privacy

At Chemery in central France
painting in the luminous
                    fading of the light
rushing colour onto canvas
– brain tissue and uncanny earthlight
and first early stars
all coinciding
before the light failed entirely
giving his picture an unearthly dimension
despite its subject
the brown colours of an old cowshed

Every evening at the same time
he'd try to make transience permanent
and three precise furrows growing
transversely on his forehead
denoted the days and weeks passing
while I stood watching
him spend youth on a nuance
of light

Only later
studying Turner Renoir Sisley Monet
Degas Pissaro and all the others
as well as our own Seven
when I began to think of
life itself as a kind of Impressionism
in the traverse of fading light
only later
in the interstices of the moment
provided by Gary
who never achieved anything very much
except perhaps a brief local celebrity
catching a glimpse of his face
in the forehead museum
to which fame alone
does not ensure entry

I.

I wake from a fever dream and find
square-assed Sairey Gamp
double-parked beside my bed:
"Have you had your nice bowel movement today?"
(I tell her half a dozen)
– and thermometers get shoved into my face
pills like cartwheels
jostle thru my innards
needles like glassy vampires
plunge into my arms
gallons and gallons of antibiotics
flood my veins
from a kinda coathanger on wheels
– a raging battle going on inside me
where all my blood pours down
in crimson cataracts
– but are the good guys winning?
I don't even know who the good guys are
holding tight with both hands
to Sairey Gamp's umbrella
which turns out to be her own gentle hand

2.

Shakespeare's old cliché:
"To be or not to be?"
– but I never thought the question
applied to me
being me I was immune
being me I was exempt from dying
and never doubted this eternity

of instants would continue
the hard unbroken carapace of self
has barred all intruders
from my private places except
that disgraceful little manikin
slouching in the brain's hallways
puffing a cigarette or maybe
marijuana the little bastard
now nowhere to be found tho
probably playing billiards
around the *medulla oblongata*
later maybe footsie
with the talent that's available
– unexpectedly he speaks to me:
"Of course you're gonna
die but not just yet"
like an organ *obbligato*
"– not just yet"

3.
Pain has entered me
under my fingernails
and through all my orifices
it screams at me to die
I am so aware of pain
the world all around me
is completely unreal
I feel myself panting
like a huge extinct beast
a sack of grey flesh panting for air
trying to breathe all the air
in the world at once
swallowing curtains furniture all
then shrinking to a bag of empty skin

eyes popping from my head
fingers become claws
— the toilet mirror
I cannot bear to see myself
whatever me that I once was
has abandoned the body here
never to see myself again
no other visit my bedside
until I feel their eyes
I cannot bear their eyes
and lie still under the earth
and sleep alone under the earth
alone in the earth

4.

Grab anything
hold onto anything
whatever made life good
whatever made life real
feeling your brain actually touch
whatever you were looking for
before you knew what that was:
until you become at least
partially that other thing
And Blake's "What is it in men that women
do require? The lineaments of gratified desire"
— those moments certainly
moments of silence when nothing could be added
to life and nothing taken away
and the moment was everything
when it seemed your face
had surrounded me like the sun
and your body surrounded me
like the living moon

and I was bathed in you
and I was drowned in you
– in the hallway someone tries the door

5.
Some time in the night
my brain had darkened
I found myself far distant from earth
lost in high nothingness
and it is a question now
whether I shall return to earth
and the doppelgänger in the hospital bed
will keep on pretending it's me –
All my loves on distant earth
seem imaginary now
my feelings for them like a story
written by another writer
– at my elbow that Other
like a friend – like a friend?
and yet someone you don't know
but someone who looks familiar
I try to see his face more clearly
but darkness swirls around his face
like fog except that it is darkness
and his clothes are the same non-colour
I want to speak to him about my indecision
whether I wish to return to that confusion
on earth with everyone rushing about
and nothing very important
and nothing that can't wait until tomorrow
and the loves that once seemed all in all
changed from moment to moment and become
only a vague discontent with myself
But nothingness? And lose everything?

– the entire world coiled tightly in my brain
the obstreperous inhabitants of this ball of mud
and all the lovely women
I ask again the question: is there no one?
– and of course my loves are there
but scattered at different points in time
almost different stars and different planets
none extend beyond their small perch in time
except as I have given them reality
But netted in my brain I draw them in
with some surprise I do feel something for them
in some surprise notice they are nearly everyone
and feel myself maudlin silly stupid
for not having realized my own feelings
except in this extremity
but there it is: I don't want to leave earth
at least not until I look once more
into their eyes and reach beyond indifference
into their hearts and minds and impossible souls
till I have remembered them beyond forgetting
– the Other turns away as if I had spoken
and darkness swirling round him scatters
the unreadable expression on his face
he nods to me and goes

Sweating I lie in the narrow bed at Saanichton
fever aches in me
antibiotics in little plastic bags
going glug-glug-glug like bad table manners
and I am standing up precariously in a small boat
in the midst of all the beer I ever drank
and cheering loudly for I don't know what
and cannot see the shore

6.

This is the earth of Lawrence
who could not bear to leave the place
and even in death his feet danced on the earth
– and do not forget those others
it's also the earth of Yeats & García Márquez
of Sakharov & Frank Scott & Margaret Laurence
Sairey Gamp and MacDiarmid's Audh
asleep in Iceland
in her resting place of stones
How could you bear to leave them here
and go where there is no remembrance?
– and all your friends those very few
you retained long enough to deserve the name
and this earth where your evolving mind
made little leaps and jumps and sideways hops
uncertain of intent or compass or direction
and reaching out from islands in time
overtook your different self like markers
pointing where you'd never been before
– how can you bear to leave them
all your selves
and never know what they might have done
or been or seemed or lost themselves in being
in your own absence in their own loneliness?

– like an organ *obbligato*
"not just yet –"

ON BEING HUMAN

When my mother went to hospital
after a fall alone in her bedroom
I was eighteen miles away
trying to build a house

I visited her later
and something in my face made her say
"I thought you'd feel terrible"
and she meant that I'd be devastated
by what had happened to her
– I wasn't feeling anything very much
at the time and I guess it showed
just thinking I'd have to travel
those eighteen miles every day
to visit her and grumbling to myself
At that moment
she had seen behind the shutters
normally drawn across the human face
and suddenly realized
there wasn't much if any
affection for her in my face
and that knowledge
was worse than her injuries

But there is no going back in time
to do anything about it now
if something wasn't done then
and nothing was
She died not much later
her mind disoriented
forgetting what happened to her

but I remember those last words
list them first
among the things I'm ashamed of
as intolerable as realizing
your whole life has been wasted
– remembering my cousin's words
about her drunken brother:
"It would have been better
if he'd never lived at all"

I remember those last words
before the fever took her mind
and the only good thing now
is thinking about those words
and she is instantly
restored to life
in my mind
and repeats the same words
"I thought you'd feel terrible"
again and again and again
          and I am still ashamed
          and I am still alive

GARDENING

I keep watching you
your serious face
and saying things sometimes
in order to see the delicate oval
mirror of yourself
change from moment to moment
like no oil painting ever did
and you all the time aware
of what I'm doing
intruding
like a lover

Then remembering
being ten years old
and hovering
every morning
over the garden
I planted and tended
for hours and days
and weeks it seemed
examining the ground
anxiously
like a mother
awaiting
her green children
child midwife
almost surprised
to see the carrots'
green fans opening
small dancers
in the wind

their whispering
so close to silence
it's like listening
underground
to the seeds loving
– and the beets
with those two leaves
sent on ahead
to ask if it's all right
for their sisters
to come as well
– and slim green tubes
of onions
push into light
astonished
at what's already there
– and I kneeling
on the damp earth
uneasy every night
before in case of
killing frost
the morning after

The analogy is inexact of course
the human face is not a garden
nor your expressions identifiable
and such intensive observation
makes you uneasy sometimes
and turn to meet my eyes
and just sometimes
tho very seldom
we know at once
what each is thinking of
and in the wonder of knowing

the night before
forget the killing frost
the morning after
that leaps the garden wall

SEASONS

Winter
in our thoughts of each other
and I remember
the way another woman looked
at me as if I were the most
least thing on earth
and I was somehow I was
my own existence ended
and summer gradually coming on
to fill my vacuum in her mind
In late winter
before the melting time
the crocus stirred preparing
underground for its spring entrance
I lessened and grew more:
all least things affect me in season
all those remnants of memory
wind-worn and transparent
seen from the other side of now
as if I were looking at you
across some kind of curtain
and you were looking at me
from another curtain
as all things lessened
and grew more

Summer was very late that year
the birds seemed bewildered
questioning each other about snow
which some had never seen before
ice rimed the shorelines

and made small tinkling sounds
as if to say welcome
but wind blew colder
and they sent messages
to relatives farther
south and said "Don't come"
It made no difference
the weasel's red eye glittered
foxes hunted and the human hunters
blew on their hands shivering
We shrugged close to the heater
and didn't speak
I would have said
"Why do you hate me?"
but it was useless
we grunted with our eyes

Let me be quite forgotten
and come to think of it
I want to be
anonymous as a raindrop
slightly off course and falling
away from the sun maybe
finding the slim wingbones
of a bird among the cedars
a bird who may have thought
"oh dear – oh dear – oh dear"
before dying
let me be quite forgotten
as snow falls from the red sun
like a thousand thousand flowers
until our tracks are covered

In 1957 when we were short of money
I was a model for a few days
at the Montreal School of Fine Arts
wearing shorts and being a boxer
for a group of twenty or so artists
They turned me in one direction
then facing the place I'd been before
so that I seemed to be fighting my ghost self
and the feeling was most peculiar
I didn't move my head only
my eyes looking into those other eyes
and felt little bits of myself
disappearing from me as they painted
and thought that if it had rained
I might have been wet internally
through all the holes they left in me
And then this Group of Seven guy
who ran the place came round
and looked at everyone's work
in which I was abstracted from me
and nodded approvingly at some of it
and didn't notice me up there
in boxer shorts
on my little wooden platform at all
And ever since then I have always
looked at things two or three times
at least to make sure they're there
and of course the guy who ran
the place isn't there any more
when I looked back to see
his name was Arthur Lismer

Rabbits running
an inch ahead of slavering dogs
do they experience intensity equivalent
to Gounod's *Faust* say
in its closing passages
as the dog's teeth click together
and the rabbit comic strip ends
in real-life death?

Our romantic human orgasm
has been likened to
the fall of Troy:
"A shudder in the loins
engenders there
The broken wall,
the burning roof and tower
And Agamemnon dead"
— Yeats lousing up
both Freud and Homer
Which is all very well
but in this small enquiry
is there a rabbit equivalent
to hitting high C
in operatic performance
the vision splendid
of a rodent future
during rabbit orgasm?

But leave off the grandiose:
is there an artistic equivalent
(apart from D.H. Lawrence)

for the tortoise's slow dance
of tumescence and detumescence
into personal oblivion
Beethoven's such-and-such concerto
sounding like tortoise nonsense
at a beach-front casino?

All great imaginings
prefigured by the word "all":
a streak of blood
in the yolk of a chicken's egg
the violin's grating nerves
shrieking in a dog's bones
warmth of heat and light
transferred to music and literature
the painter's passion
interchangeable with nerve endings
of fish and fur and fowl
of course deity
would experience all this too
wakeful on his/her golden throne
and to imagine it is also
to hear the soundless bellow
of eternity
chipping away at a china teacup
and the rabbit's cry . . .

ATOMIC LULLABY

No second spring again
for you and I my love
our half life is thirty years
there is no second coming

We stood on Mount Moriah
counting from one to ten
and slowly we stopped our caring
or pretending we ever did

Say love when the ice gnaws deeper
say love when the fire eats down
could we waste a thought on each other
have we time for romance then

Our myth is the cherished nonsense
that somewhere something survives
and the minds in our dying bodies
glow deep in a stranger's eyes

Sleep – would that have been better?
It is so – it becomes the same
when stars rush out at evening
my dust forgets your name

To pass on the street without knowing
well that won't happen to us
but the most we can be to each other
is someone who looks like someone

We were flesh but our hearts were shadows
we sent them off on their own
to a place where the stones are strangers
but bone speaketh to bone

TOUCHINGS

Lying in darkness before sleep
my hand reaching for your hand
that is waiting for me or not waiting
and reaching out my mind to other minds
– Yeats dead in southern France
his body exhumed after the war
and ferried home on an Irish destroyer
buried again near Sligo under Ben Bulben
Yeats whispering under his blanket of earth:
>"– the best lack all conviction
>and the worst,
>are full of passionate intensity"
and I think of Mulroney
not the least of my detestations

It's like free fall in space I suppose
to feel your mind free itself
from your body and the illusion
of boundaries
– following MacLeish's darkness
around the world:
>"And now at Kermanshah the gate
>Dark empty and the withered grass
>And through the twilight now the late
>Few travellers in the westward pass
>And Baghdad darken and the bridge
>Across the silent river gone –"

– the hand in my hand grows restless
cold fingers release me
those other minds again imminent

– I visit Lawrence in Italy
and we chuckle over that he-goat
of his climbing an olive tree:
>"– like some hairy horrid God the Father
>in a William Blake imagination"

Of course it's a game of remembering
and all the limbo-faces draw near
to gaze down on you like Layton's ex-wives
along with your own old girl friends
– W.J. Turner whispering in your ear:
>"I have stood upon a hill
>and trembled like a man in love
>a man in love I was and
>could not speak and could not move"

I shift my heavy body in bed restlessly
sometimes there is no handholding
depending on whether we're on good terms
– a perceptible coldness?
>>The mind wanders
away to Auden in his house of earth:
>"Time that is intolerant
>of the brave and innocent
>and indifferent in a week
>to a beautiful physique
>worships language and forgives
>everyone by whom it lives –"
– deleted by Auden and not to be found
anywhere except in his early books
and migawd I should be so literary

Switch to Rilke before Duino:
"Whoever has no house now will never have one

whoever is alone will stay alone"
        – now the faces of all my friends
ride through the night on broomsticks
                        and ballpoints
except Margaret A. on her hobbyhorse:
"Leeuwenhock peered through his magic window
and in a puddle glimpsed the tiny grain
of firmament that was before Adam"

– and these midnight touchings
are my own magic window
– in darkness the great stone of the world
sent wobbling through space
whose surface we cling to
– in our rumpled beds
like small untidy coffins
drifting among the cold lights in the sky
as if we had always known
where we were going

Reach out your hand my love

DEITY

In grey weather along the Ionian coast
we found a god near Bodrum
– it had no body only a stone head
smothered in grass by a ruined temple
and picking off this tangled blindfold
uncovered a face momentarily uncertain
of its own identity in the absence of believers
– then the eyes seemed to find us
standing knee-deep in grass
bending over whatever it was

The Greeks were long-vanished when we
came here and for centuries
our newly discovered god was forgotten
but now our eyes are compelled
by those other eyes
as if we turned to see a grey fire
burning along the Aegean littoral
and dancing figures in the grey light
and cannot look into that burning long
and yet having awakened the god
we cannot turn away

Turkey

Spring with Pablo Neruda
and I peering out the bathroom
window at some imaginary
female and he sez to her
"I want to do to you what
spring does to the cherry trees"
whereat I am so jealous of
his metaphors I point out that
no imaginary human female could
behave like a cherry tree does
which shuts him up just briefly
and I draw his attention to two
bushtits nestbuilding in our lilac
bush with a rufous hummingbird the
size of a gold thumbnail watching
domestic activities avidly then
he starts to spin round and round
inside that lilac bush like a
small rotor or prayerwheel for
midgets going
zing-zing-zing soundless as
a cardinal picking his nose
with a gold thumbnail and
bragging at the same time
"Can you do this? Canyoucanyoucanyou?"
Obviously no this great corpus of
unwritten poems can't even
circumnavigate a toilet bowl
without my wife's astrolabe
and my astonishment at this goofy
bird explodes out of the bathroom

window in full view of all and
sundry whereupon
hummingbirds bushtits and Pablo
are shocked out of existence and
repair to the heights of
Machu Picchu searching for
some mislaid condor eggs

Not like Shelley's "Adonais"
when Keats had "gone
where all things bright and fair
descend" –
I'd never think of Tom like that
talk about purity and dawn
and that kinda bullshit
Anyway
forty days after his death
there's a lump of sorrow somewhere
in my head I can't get rid of

The others: Gwen Acorn bp Nichol
Frank Scott Bronwen & Margaret
the list goes on and on
the world's obituary
but Tom is a sort of culmination
a man I took for granted
and figured I'd leave *him* here
not vice versa
and now I feel desolate
as if half the world's population
all of them my friends
had made off somewhere
and never waved goodbye
but then
whoever gets to wave goodbye?

No mention here
of Tom's "accomplishments"
irrelevant to this lump of sorrow

nor his magnetic personality
which he didn't have anyway
– just say that he joins
all those others
the named and nameless
people who went before
back to the stone-age men
who did those cave paintings
even Keats in a Roman cemetery
(but not Shelley's version)
coughing out his lungs
in England and Italy
Sakharov and Lawrence
and those Neanderthals
who placed flowers in graves
earth itself sown deep with bones
All of which doesn't mean much
for I have this sorrow
which is not beautiful
or noble or pure
has nothing to do
with stained-glass windows
or droning preachers
sorrow is a lump of stuff
the stuff of everyday living
gurgle of a beer bottle
sound of a door closing
typewriter blatting away
natter of cars somewhere
orchids in the Brazilian jungle
which don't exist
because I'm not there
to bear witness?
– sorrow for the dead is

premonitory to your own
departure for a place
where there is no one
waiting for you
– and this collection
of hen-scratches on paper
must be for Tom's friends
all those living
who feel his absence
as a lump of sorrow
demonstrating here my own
extreme sensitivity?
making it perhaps
bearable for me?
Goddammit
all this is a lie
a friend dead is unbearable
and should be unbearable
and these words are meant to
make things easy for myself
but nothing is easy
I wouldn't want to feel any different
I want to feel awful
and I do

WANDERING THROUGH TROY

To actually be there
hover between myth and reality
earth chemicals identical
with Ameliasburgh or nearly
same time stream
various co-ordinates checking
ticking off the list of names
the way he thought/the way I think
my imagination churning away
and pleased with myself
Sure it's kinda silly
but you feel it
the Troy-Homer-Achilles deal
the sweat and the watchers on either hand
a great roar of chariots
without axle grease
Priam and Agamemnon
with death-botched reflexes
death two huge eyes
watching you indifferently
whispering soon enough Soon Enough
and Achilles
waking up in his tent
scratching himself
trying to remember
if he'd killed anyone
since yesterday

And stumble from city to city
all nine of them
all the different levels

jammed into each other
and you almost expect
to find human leftovers
from the instant between
one town and another
– arriving here bewildered
a little girl from the Iron Age
hugging her doll
and heat waves rising
among the broken stone

WANTING

I wanted to say wait
when you were looking back at me
when time stopped for that moment
and I kept looking at you forever
I wanted to say wait

I wanted to hear your voice again
on the phone you sounded happy
but the party line was crowded
prairie and mountain were listening
when I wanted to hear your voice

I wanted to write a letter
in which I would say everything
but it seemed as though the empty continent
was soaking up all my unsaid things

I wanted to remember
the you that was so entirely you
that I could never be mistaken
seeing you a thousand miles away
but it was someone else

And I wanted to re-live the moment
that owed nothing to before and after
the you that blotted out me
and yet did not lessen me
I wanted to
but I have forgotten how

GLACIER SPELL

Ice – islands archipelagos continents
worlds of ice
stretching north and holding the sea prisoner
wriggling uneasily in the moon's hypnosis
– and meltwater drains at the glacier's south
where a smaller sea reflects its monster parent
east and west a blue witch-light
spreads into darkness
And year by year the ice recedes
an inch or a foot on the sun's yardstick
yielding entombed creatures thawing slowly
till ice unlocks them
and they tumble from the shoulder-breech
with earth regained they tremble and shudder
appear to take a step then sink to their knees
suffering a double life and a double death
while the ice rings with a dumb chanting

As the sun strengthens a slender line of green
paints itself crookedly at the glacier's foot
and plant faces turn away from the cold
– when rains come a hundred miles of ice
and a thousand miles of sky join in
the roar of drainage to a southbound river
a sound heard by no one
– only a wandering hunter
outcast from his tribe
a man with demons in his heart
unexpectedly not at home
in the great sky rooms of earth

Time speeds and slows
moves in the altering shapes of stillness
speeding to plant a forest
slowing to welcome a bird
waiting for the first beast
while the glacier pretends it isn't there
but shitting lateral moraines
– a brown man and a brown woman
day eyes peering at night eyes
of animals outside
the fire's cave of red light
through the black and white door
where fear waits

Do not touch words to what has no name
or feel the place of wandering stones with eyes
the beast we hunt must not be said
its smell rides under the wind
its face remembers our faces

THE FARM IN LITTLE IRELAND

– Renfrew County

All the big wild emotions
that ramp and roar in the bloodstream
love hate fear jealousy
and those feelings that evoke
Hobbes' "sudden glory" of laughter
             they seem faded here
but there remains a sullenness
like ground mist
rising . . .

The 40 acres old Wannamaker
and his sons cleared
on the 200-acre farm
are grown up with brushwood
even humpback piles of rocks
horses dragged here on stone boats
have green hats
             the old log house
with asphalt siding rots slowly
porcupines chew at the backhouse
hungry for salt
inside the house pine steps
to upper bedrooms are worn
thin by dead feet
only the raised tough knots
in boards resist time

Impossible there shouldn't be
some resentment at new owners
who bought with money
the lifelong sweat and pain

of old Wannamaker and his sons
and must have made them feel useless
even to themselves
– but am I inventing such emotions
to survive when flesh is dust
and dust here is everywhere?

– grey ghosts in overalls
meander through house and meadows
where the bent grass
a bear slept on last night
is slowly springing upright
hair prickling at the back of my neck
from this excited melodrama
– an ancient rag doll in the stairwell
reminds me of vanished children
but one eye is missing from the doll
and the other button eye
blames me for the lost one

REASSESSMENT

I thought you'd stopped being beautiful
but I was wrong
you haven't stopped
and now
in order to hold
my feelings in check
halt the mental process so to speak
slow down the growing physical manifestations
I imagine you with your lower
intestine coiled and looped around your neck
(nobody looks good with the lower
intestine coiled around their neck)
in order to stop
being in love
again
which is
fairly
ridiculous
at age
75
most people would agree

Just stand there
for a casual moment
observing in yourself
what others have noticed before me
since the condition is fairly well documented
how everything stops moving
around her luminous face
and nothing is casual any more
you can't breathe

But it's late now
and I've booked passage
on that black ship
mentioned by Lawrence
and start to pick my way
along the docks
among rigid mesmerized people
looking in many different directions
and can't see me
just before I go on board
reading the passenger list
cracking a joke with the captain
although he seems singularly uncommunicative
perhaps the pressure of his duties
winking at the chief steward
and sailing off
for a last holiday

BIRDS

Coming awake early in the morning
with light only a suspicion
of greyness somewhere
listening to them
– their voices break through the quiet
become silver threads in the air
with stress and non-stress like a poem
with bird-vowels and bird-consonants
their language otherworldly
they remain in this world
but keep singing
about the other one

And me
disparate things in my mind
Bathsheba at her bath
Susanna and the Elders
Achilles
flies alighting on bodies after a battle
that great hole in the world
into which the past descends
and the birds
singing somewhere else

THE EXACT MOMENT

— for Margaret

Three bushels of grapes to clean
a legacy from Roblin Lake
bubbling in the tiny kitchen
like a spillage of whispers
Squirrels walking upsidedown
on screens of windows
— yellow red and green leaves outside
deciding what to do when wind comes
Days getting so short
they seem no more than the click of a camera
— a tall crane fumbles heavy weights
out the side window like a gigantic mantis

— nothing will ever move again
after these words

TO —

To the you that has been given some twenty
pounds of added flesh
– I have made room for this added you in my mind
and love that too

To the throat and neck that were once a column
of light holding up the moon
has been added little noughts and crosses of webbing
like to an earth pattern during the long hot days
before the end of summer
– and the clear luminous mirror of the sky
that was your face has been examined by God
and all the gods and given shadows
here and there that the sons of men
may look upon you and not lose their vision

And the mind that is both fearful of nothing
and fearless of everything has grown and become
lovely and earthly and yet beyond our soiled planet
its innocence the wisdom of things newborn
before corruption has entered their minds and bodies
and directed them to walk toward their death

– to see everything and to realize the best and worst
of everything
is to love and not forget

Shanidar 1
"One of the best preserved burials:
another male, aged between 30 & 45.
Bones revealed a plethora of serious
but healed fractures:
crushing blow to left side of head,
fracturing the eye socket –"
Purdy
Skull fracture in 1940
during RCAF tenure
caused by diving into shallow
end of swimming pool
at CFB Trenton
Shanidar 1
"– massive blow to right side
of body that so seriously damaged
the right arm that it became
withered and useless –"
Purdy
Helping Eurithe down ice-covered
hill in winter: fractured left elbow
– torn ligaments in left arm
from lugging dehumidifier downstairs
Shanidar 1
"– right foot and lower right leg
also damaged –"
Purdy
– damaged nerves in feet
with progressive numbness
creeping up both legs
plus probable fractured kneecap

caused by fall on aforementioned hill
causing lameness at later date
– also mental retardation caused by
deleterious intake and outflow
of bad poems
(Eurithe: "Serves you right!")
Shanidar 1
"As Solecki argued,
someone so devastatingly injured
could not possibly have survived
without care and sustenance –"
Purdy
Uh – thanks Eurithe –
Shanidar 1
Death
Purdy
So what else is new?

FRAGMENTS

I loved being alive
to stand between earth and sky
in springtime
a great organ playing in your bones
when earth moves
under your feet
over the long Sundays of our lives

– to feel your insides changing
                    and writhe from loss
and knowing the loss has added
to you and what you are
and clinging to life
that makes such gifts

– to feel
that your own absence may be counted
a continual presence
an onward movement
to change the future
where you are entirely unknown

– to feel your brain
lifting to stand on tip-toe
your feet pushing against the clouds

– to climb the steps of your own writing
and fall off at the highest point
and know that in falling far enough
discover what you were climbing for
and fall short of the sun

– to feel your body crumble
as the high places of earth crumble
the Athenian Acropolis and Machu Picchu
and join them as an idea
springing to life
in flesh and stone

Poems are such a mixture of the imagination and fact that I think the end result might be taken as fiction. However, the following notes do indicate the basic ingredients of a few of these poems.

*

"Grosse Isle": The name of an island in the St. Lawrence River, some thirty miles downstream from Quebec City. It was a quarantine station for cholera and typhus victims between 1832 and 1937.

"Capitalistic Attitudes": From *Moths in the Iron Curtain*, a small edition in 1979.

"Chac Mool at Chichen Itza": Chac Mool is the Mayan rain god.

"In the Desert": From *The Woman on the Shore*. The poem is revised here.

"Earle Birney in Hospital": In 1988 or thereabouts Earle Birney suffered a stroke. I visited him a couple of times at the hospital, in company with his wife, Wailan, and my own wife. I had known Earle well before his illness, and to see him like this was painful: he did not recognize me.

"The Freezing Music": A different version of the title poem of *The Woman on the Shore*, 1990.

"The Booby Hop": The blue-footed booby in the Galapagos Islands is one of the stupidest birds in existence, evidence for this being its lack of fear of human beings. The booby collects brilliant objects, does a mating dance in season, admires its feet, and is often the victim of aerial raids by frigate birds.

"Stan Rogers": The Maritimes folksinger died in an Air Canada fire on the ground at Cincinnati Airport in 1983.

"Procne into Swallow": In Greek mythology, Procne was married to Tereus, King of Thrace. When Tereus raped Procne's attractive sister, Philomela, he cut her tongue out afterwards for fear she would reveal his crime. But Philomela was able to tell her sister what had happened by embroidering the story on her robes. Procne, out of her mind with rage, killed her own son, Itys, and served him to Tereus for dinner. Whereupon the two sisters were pursued by Tereus with a drawn sword. However, before he could do any damage, the benevolent gods changed Philomela into a nightingale, Procne into a swallow, Itys into a goldfinch, and Tereus into a hoopoe. And they live forever in Greek mythology.

"Concerning Ms. Atwood": This poem, among other things, deals with fame and celebrity. I hasten to add: it is not meant to impugn Ms. Atwood's character in any way, nor that of her admirers. She read an earlier version, viewed it calmly, and allowed it to stand.

"Incident Involving William Blake": This is a verbatim quote of a letter from Blake to a friend. It depicts an unfamiliar side to Blake's character, which is one of my reasons for including it here as a "found poem." Blake, described as a "miniature painter," was charged with high treason. At his trial, January 11, 1804, he was cleared of all charges.

"Touchings": The quotes are from memory, and would be verbatim only if my memory was perfect (which it isn't).

"The Crucifix Across the Mountains": There is an old road in Germany, once travelled by emperors and high church dignitaries. Its route is from Munich to Innsbruck, Austria, and on across the Alps to Italy. D.H. Lawrence tramped this road with his wife, Frieda, shortly before the First World War. At intervals along the road Lawrence noticed small crucifixes, each of them accompanied by wooden carvings of Christ, each a reflection of the human character of its particular region, as depicted by local sculptors. My poem is taken from DHL's essay of the same title.

"Seasons": Also slightly revised. It was overlooked when my *Collected* was being put together in 1986. Since this is probably my last book of poems, I don't want it overlooked again.

"Atomic Lullaby": Extracted from a much longer poem in *The Stone Bird*, 1981. Mount Moriah, some thirty miles north of Belleville, Ontario, was proposed as an atomic waste site in the late 1970s. This poem too is slightly revised.

"Neanderthal": The quotations are from the *New York Times Book Review*, July 4, 1983.

* * *

I would like to acknowledge the magazines where some of these poems first appeared: *Acta Victoriana*, *Borealis*, *Canadian Forum*, *Carousel*, *Inkwell*, *The Idler*, *Quarry*, the Al Purdy issue of *Essays in Canadian Writing* (ECW Press), and *Slow Dancer* (England). Thanks also to the Canada Council and the Ontario Arts Council, and most especially to Stan Dragland, the publisher's editor; and to Sam Solecki for the same reason.

AWP